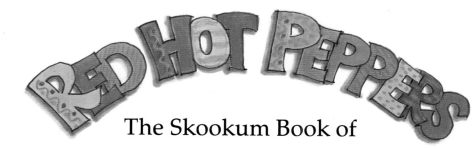

RED HOT PEPPERS

The Skookum Book of
Jump Rope Games, Rhymes, and Fancy Footwork

Text by
Bob Boardman

Illustrations by
Diane Boardman

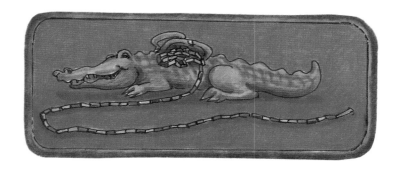

Sasquatch Books

Skookum
Products & Services

Published by Sasquatch Books in cooperation with the Skookum Jump Rope Company

Printed in Hong Kong

Library of Congress Cataloging in Publication Data

Boardman, Bob, 1947–
    Red hot peppers: the Skookum book of jump rope games, rhymes, and
    fancy footwork / Bob Boardman; illustrations by Diane Boardman.
        p.   cm.
    Includes bibliographical references (p.60).
    ISBN 0-912365-74-9: $8.95
    1. Rope skipping—Juvenile literature. 2. Jump rope rhymes—
    Juvenile literature. I. Boardman, Diane, ill. II. Title.
    GV498.B63   1993
    796.2—dc20   92-96835
                                                        CIP
                                                         AC

Sasquatch Books
1931 Second Avenue
Seattle, WA 98101
(206) 441-5555

Skookum Jump Rope Company
P.O. Box 97
Port Townsend, WA 98368
1-800-255-9526

The high skip,
The sly skip,
The skip like a feather.
The long skip,
The strong skip,
The skip all together.
The slow skip,
The toe skip,
The skip double-double.
The fast skip,
The last skip,
The skip against trouble!
　　　　　—Eleanor Farjeon

Contents

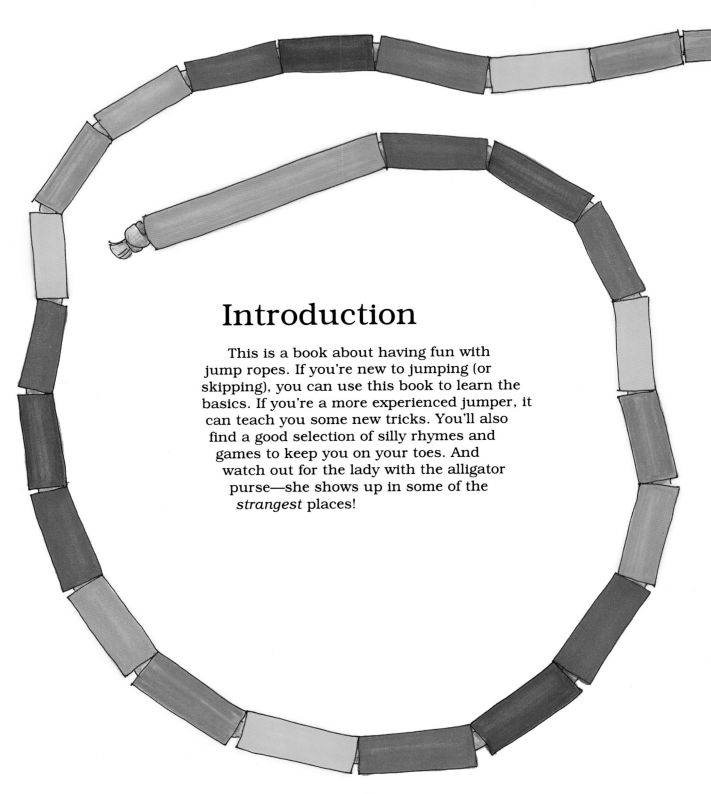

Introduction

This is a book about having fun with jump ropes. If you're new to jumping (or skipping), you can use this book to learn the basics. If you're a more experienced jumper, it can teach you some new tricks. You'll also find a good selection of silly rhymes and games to keep you on your toes. And watch out for the lady with the alligator purse—she shows up in some of the *strangest* places!

Skipping Through History

No one knows who invented rope skipping, but it's probably been around for a very long time. It's easy to imagine the children of Egyptian or Chinese rope makers jumping over strands of hemp that their parents had twisted together. A picture on an ancient Greek vase shows a girl skipping over a vine.

By the 1700s, rope skipping was a game for boys. Skipping was considered unladylike, and the long skirts that girls wore made it hard for them to jump.

A hundred years later, skirts were shorter, and more and more girls began to skip. In time, skipping became mostly a girls' activity.

Today, more boys and girls than ever are skipping rope. And not just on playgrounds. Rope skipping has gone big-time. Jumping teams compete in international tournaments sponsored by the American Double Dutch League and the International Rope Skipping Organization. Some of these competitions are televised, and thousands of kids participate.

More than a million boys and girls have learned the basics of skipping through the Jump Rope for Heart Program, sponsored by the American Heart Association.

So you can skip with your friends for fun, or join a team and tour the world. The sky's the limit for today's jumpers!

Rhymes and Jumping

For hundreds of years, rhymes and skipping have gone together. Your parents and grandparents can probably remember a few of the rhymes they jumped to as children. Some rhymes have been passed from generation to generation and from country to country around the world. New rhymes are being invented every day.

Toward the back of this book you'll find a few of our favorite rhymes and information about where to find more.

Some of the rhymes are very old, some come from faraway countries, and some are here just because we like them. We hope you will too.

Jumping for Fitness

Jumping rope is fun. It's also very good exercise. One reason skipping is so popular today is that it's such a good way to keep in shape. Many fitness experts consider rope jumping to be the perfect workout. It exercises the legs, the arms, and the cardiovascular system (the network made up of your heart and blood vessels). Skipping for 15 minutes is as good for you as running 2 miles or bicycling 3 miles!

You can keep jumping rope all your life. It doesn't take any fancy equipment, and you can do it almost anywhere.

You may be jumping rope for the fun of it, but isn't it nice to know that it's one of the best exercises you can do?

Before You Jump...

You'll Need a Rope

There are many different kinds of jump ropes. At the Skookum Jump Rope Company, we make beaded ropes and single-strand "speed ropes." Some jumpers like beaded ropes because they're easier to control at slow speeds. This can be handy when you're learning new tricks. Beaded ropes also make a distinctive "click" when they hit the ground. That can make it easier to set a good rhythm.

Speed ropes are lighter and quicker than other ropes. Some jumpers think they're more comfortable to use, especially for tougher tricks. But you don't need a fancy rope to start jumping. Any piece of rope or cord or heavy clothesline, knotted at the ends, will work just fine.

Experiment with different kinds of rope for different kinds of jumping. The best rope is the one you feel most comfortable with.

How Long a Rope?

How long a rope you need depends on what sort of jumping you'll be doing. The length will be different for single, double, and long-rope styles of jumping. A rope that's a little too long is better than one that's too short. You can always shorten it by tying knots at the ends or a few inches below the handles.

For Single Jumping
• Hold an end of the rope in each hand, and stand on the middle. The ends should come up to your armpits.

For Side-by-Side Jumping
• With you and a friend both standing on the middle of the rope, the ends should come up to your armpits.

For the Wheel, Traveling, and Jumping with a Partner
• The ends of the rope should come up to your shoulders when you're standing on the middle.

Be Nice to Your Body

Any comfortable clothing is fine for jumping rope. A good pair of tennis shoes or running shoes will cushion your feet. If possible, jump on a surface that has some "give" in it. Wood or tile floors, rubber mats, or carpets are easier on your joints than asphalt or concrete.

Remember, jumping can be strenuous exercise. It's always good to warm up a little before starting. Touch your toes, do some jumping jacks, or run in place for a few minutes before you jump.

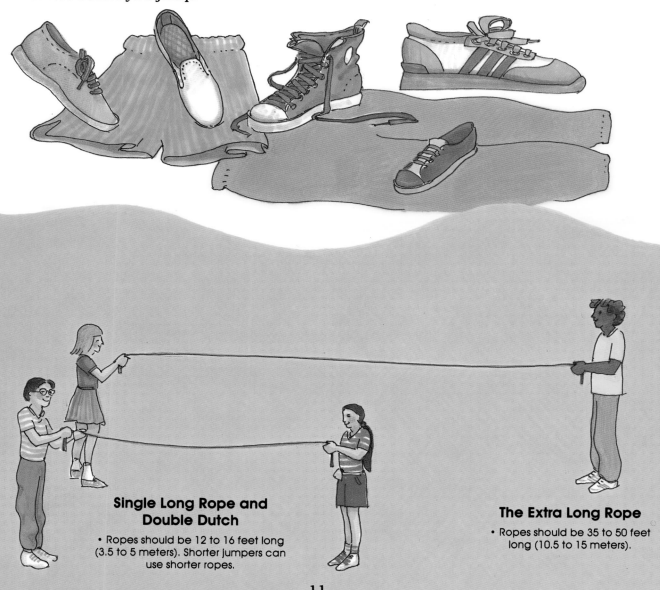

Single Long Rope and Double Dutch

• Ropes should be 12 to 16 feet long (3.5 to 5 meters). Shorter jumpers can use shorter ropes.

The Extra Long Rope

• Ropes should be 35 to 50 feet long (10.5 to 15 meters).

Getting Started

To learn the most basic style of jumping, hold the ends of the rope in both hands with your elbows close to your body and your arms bent. If your rope has handles, your thumbs should be on top of them.

Start with the rope behind your heels and swing it over your head. When it comes to your feet, jump just high enough to get over it.

Jump on the balls of your feet (the big pad of your foot behind your toes), with your feet together and your knees slightly bent. At first, you can include a little bounce step between skips. As you pick up speed, though, try to do a single jump each time the rope passes under your feet.

Your hands should be making small circles, but keep your elbows close to your body.

Try It Backward

Once you can do the Basic Jump, try swinging the rope in the other direction, from front to back. Jump as the rope comes under your feet from behind.

Just You

These are tricks you can do by yourself with a jump rope. They're arranged from easy to hard, but you can jump in anywhere. As you learn the tricks, you can put them together into routines. The tricks are like words: See what sort of story you can write with your jump rope.

Simple Tricks

Remember, if you have trouble doing any of these, put down the rope and just practice the footwork. After a few minutes, try it again with the rope. Begin each of these tricks with a few Basic Jumps.

Side Swing

This isn't a jump at all. It's just swinging the rope from side to side.

1. Move both hands to your right side.
2. Spin the rope around so that it touches the floor.
3. Move your hands to the left side and swing the rope around again.

Side Swing and Jump

The same side-to-side swing, but with a jump in the middle.

1. Do a Side Swing on your right.
2. Move your left hand to your left side, open the rope, and do a regular jump.
3. Move both hands to the left and do a Side Swing on your left.
4. Move your right hand to your right side and do another regular jump.

Side-to-Side—the Ski Jump

While you're doing the Basic Jump, try jumping sideways 6 inches (15 centimeters) to the left. On the next swing of the rope, jump the same distance to the right. Keep alternating side to side with each swing.

Forward and Back

While you're doing the Basic Jump, try jumping forward 6 inches (15 centimeters). On the next swing of the rope, jump the same distance backward. Alternate jumping backward and forward with each swing.

Side Straddle

This is a lot like doing a jumping jack, except that you swing the rope under you each time you move your feet. Do a few Basic Jumps and then:

1. Land with your feet about 12 inches (30 centimeters) apart.

2. On the next swing of the rope, land with your feet together again.

3. With each swing, move your feet apart, together, apart.

Straddle Cross

This one is just like the Side Straddle, except that instead of bringing your feet together, you *cross* them.

The Twist

1. On the first swing of the rope, jump and twist your hips to the right. Try to move only your hips—keep your shoulders facing forward.

2. On the next jump, twist your hips to the left.

3. Twist back to the right.

15

Not-So-Simple Tricks

...then again, you might not think these are hard at all. Remember, it always helps to slow things down or work on only one part of a trick at a time. Again, begin each trick with a few Basic Jumps.

Double-Under

In this trick, you swing the rope *twice* each time you jump.

1. Jump a little higher than you usually do.
2. Swing the rope really fast, so it goes under your feet twice between jumps. Use wrist action to whip the rope around.
3. Jump again and repeat the two-swings-to-one-jump rhythm.
4. Try doing a Double-Under on every third jump, then every second jump, and finally every time.

Criss-Cross

A neat trick and not too tough at all.

1. Bring the rope forward and cross your arms. Make sure to bring your hands all the way across the front of your body, as if you were giving yourself a hug. Your elbows should almost touch.
2. Swing the rope and jump. Then uncross your arms and jump again.

Jogging Step

This is just like running in place, except that you jump after each step.

1. Hop on your left foot, raising the other as if you were running.
2. Jump over the rope as you hop.
3. Change feet and hop over the rope with your right foot.

Can-Can

This is a four-step trick.

1. Jump on your left foot, lifting your right knee.
2. On the next swing of the rope, jump with your feet together.
3. Jump again on your left foot, kicking your right knee in front of your body.
4. Jump with your feet together again. Do the same trick with your left leg.

180-Degree Turn

When you do this turn, you'll find yourself jumping backward (with the rope coming over your head from front to back).

1. Move your hands to your left side and swing the rope in a circle to the side.

2. Pivot your body to the left a half-turn.

3. Open your hands and bring the rope over your head from front to back. You are now jumping with the rope going backward.

This sounds harder than it really is. Try it slowly at first, just walking through the movements without actually jumping. When you start jumping, the turns can be done very slowly. Once you get the hang of it, it's a lot of fun.

360-Degree Turn

This is a series of two turns. After turning around to the back, you come around to the front again.

1. Do the 180-Degree Turn. You're now jumping backward.

2. As the rope comes over your head, pivot halfway around and swing the rope down in front of you. Now you're jumping forward.

19

Even Trickier Tricks

It isn't hard to figure out *how* to do these tricks, but it will take some practice to be able to do them smoothly. Begin each trick with a few Basic Jumps.

Leg Over

The tough part of this one is getting your arm under your leg far enough that the rope swings freely. Try jumping higher than usual.

1. As the rope is coming forward, hop on your left foot.

2. At the same time, raise your right leg and reach your right arm as far under it as you can.

3. Jump over the rope a few times on your left foot.

4. Getting out: As the rope swings over your head, pull your right arm out from under your leg. Then, with both arms, pull the rope over to your right side.

5. Do a Side Swing; then bring the rope back to the front and continue with the Basic Jump. Now try the whole thing on the other foot.

20

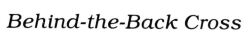

Behind-the-Back Cross

When you do this trick, hold the very ends of your rope, to give you a little more length.

1. Just after the rope passes under your feet as you do the Basic Jump, cross both your arms behind your back. Keep your hands at hip level.
2. Jump with your arms crossed behind your back. *Remember to turn the rope with only your wrists as you jump.*
3. Uncross your arms and keep jumping.

Front-Back Cross

1. Move your hands to the right, as if you were going to do a Side Swing, but then let your right hand continue around your back until it has crossed to the far left side.
2. Jump a few times.
3. Bring your hands back to the front and do the Basic Jump.
4. Repeat the cross starting from the other side.

You and a Friend

These are jumping tricks you can do with a
friend. Some use one rope and others use two.

One Rope

Side-by-Side

1. Stand next to your friend, with each of you
   holding an end of the rope in your outside
   hand.
2. Swing the rope and do the Basic Jump
   together. You can do a number of tricks in this
   position, like the Side Straddle, Side-to-Side,
   and Forward and Back.
3. Vary the trick by turning the rope backward or
   by facing in opposite directions.

Turn In, Turn Out

In this trick, you go from being a jumper to
being a turner, and then back again.

1. Begin jumping side by side with your
   friend.
2. Make either a quarter-turn backward or
   a three-quarter turn forward, keeping
   your rope hand on the side of you that's
   closest to your friend. You are now
   outside the rope, turning it for your
   friend.
3. Reverse the turn to get back inside. Now
   it's your friend's turn.

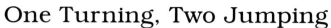

One Turning, Two Jumping

This is a great way to jump together, especially if you're jumping with someone who's not the same size as you. The bigger person turns the rope. These tricks work best with a little longer rope. If you're the taller person, when you stand on the rope, the ends should reach the top of your shoulders.

The Basic Jump

1. Both partners face forward, with the turner standing behind the other. Stay close together.

2. Do the Basic Jump with both partners jumping at the same time.

Variations

• The front partner can do a 360-Degree Turn in one, two, three, or four jumps.

• Both partners can do Side Straddles or Side-to-Sides.

• The front partner can jump in and out of the rope, or go "around-the-world" by jumping all the way around the turner.

Two Ropes

Unison Jumping

You and a friend can each do your own single-rope tricks in unison, side by side. It can be fun to put tricks together and work up a "routine."

Trading Handles

This trick requires two jumpers and two single-length ropes. You stand side by side with your friend, but each of you hold the inside end of the other's rope. Now begin jumping at the same time. You can do most of your single-rope tricks in this position.

The Wheel

This way of jumping is as much fun to look at as it is to do. Ropes a little longer than usual help. The ends of your rope should reach the top of your shoulders when you're standing on it.

The arm movements take some getting used to, so here's an exercise to help get you started.

1. Stand between two friends, with all three of you facing forward. Hold one end of each rope, and let your friends hold the other ends with their outside hands.

2. Swing your arms in a swimming motion, so that one rope is high when the other is low. As you swing the ropes, your friends jump. Keep the rhythm slow and steady.

3. Stop and trade places, so that everyone gets a chance to be in the middle and on both ends.

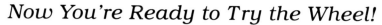

Now You're Ready to Try the Wheel!

Begin with a two-person Wheel:

1. Stand side by side and trade inside handles. The ropes should be behind your feet.

2. Start by swinging the rope that is the farthest back.

3. When the first rope is overhead, start swinging the second rope.

4. Turn the ropes slowly and take a little bounce step after each jump. One partner should always be up when the other is down. If you find yourselves jumping at the same time, you've lost the Wheel and should try again.

Once you've mastered the basic steps, you can add more friends and more ropes. Three is lovely, four is spectacular, and five is unbelievable!

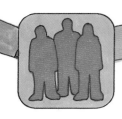

You and Two Friends

This chapter will introduce you to jumping with one or two long ropes. Jumping with one long rope is great for games and rhymes. Jumping with two long ropes is called "Double Dutch," and it's about as fast and exciting as rope skipping can get!

Most of the skills you learn jumping with a single long rope can be applied to Double Dutch jumping too.

Turning the Rope

Turning the rope may not look very exciting, but turners (or "enders") are actually very important. Good turning makes good jumping much easier. Here are some tips to help you be a good turner:

1. Hold the rope with your thumb on top and your wrist locked.

2. Keep your upper arm stationary. Rotate the lower arm at the elbow.

3. Turn the rope so that a few feet in the middle of it touch the ground.

Entering the Rope

To jump, you first have to get into the middle of the turning rope. If the rope hits the ground and moves *away* from you, that's called entering by the "front door." This is the easiest way to get into the rope. If the spinning rope hits the ground and moves *toward* you, that's called entering by the "back door." It's a bit trickier.

Front Door

Stand next to the turner's shoulder. As the rope hits the ground and moves away, run to the middle and jump as the rope moves around again.

Back Door

As the rope reaches the top, run in quickly. You'll have to take a big jump over the rope as it comes under your feet.

29

The Basic Jump

1. Jump just high enough to clear the rope.
2. Add a little bounce step between jumps. Unless, of course, you're jumping "Red Hot Peppers!" Hot Peppers means the rope is turning very fast. Red Hot Peppers means it's turning even faster.

Exiting the Rope

After a jump, take a last jump toward a turner and step out. Don't hesitate—but don't run out, either. You should aim as close as you can to the turner's shoulder when you leave the rope.

Tricks

Because a long rope turns so slowly, it's great to use for tricks. You can do most of the tricks you learned with the short rope while jumping in the long rope. Try doing the Side Straddle, Side-to-Side, Forward and Back, or the Twist. Try doing 360-Degree Turns in four jumps, then two jumps, and then only one!

Short Rope Inside a Long Rope

This is lots of fun. The turners should be sure the long rope is going high over the jumper's head. The jumper may want to use a rope that's shorter than usual.

1. Enter the long rope carrying the short rope with you.
2. Start jumping your short rope in rhythm with the long rope. Now you're jumping over both ropes at the same time.
3. Stop jumping your short rope, take a few more jumps over the long one, and exit.

30

Double Dutch

Double Dutch is an exciting two-rope game. The enders turn two ropes at the same time, like an eggbeater. The ropes are turned inward, toward each other. For the jumper this means jumping twice as fast, while doing all sorts of tricks.

Double Dutch has been played for years, especially by children on the streets of big cities such as New York. In 1974, a New York City police detective named David Walker organized the first Double Dutch tournament. Since then, competitive Double Dutch jumping has caught on like wildfire all around the country and the world.

Double Dutch tournaments have become international events. In 1992 more than 250,000 boys and girls competed in the American Double Dutch League's World Tournament. The finals were broadcast on television.

Getting Started at Double Dutch

In this book, we'll explain how to turn the ropes, how to enter and leave the ropes, and how to do a few tricks. But that's just the beginning of what's possible with Double Dutch. World-class routines include acrobatics, dancing, and footwork so fancy it's almost hard to believe.

If you'd like more information or want to start your own Double Dutch team, you can write to:

American Double Dutch League
4220 Eads St. N.E.
Washington, DC 20019

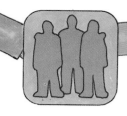

Turning the Ropes

Turning is the key to Double Dutch. Entering or leaving the ropes is difficult unless the turners do their jobs well, and jumpers depend on good turning to do their tricks. Good turning takes practice, but the effort is worth it.

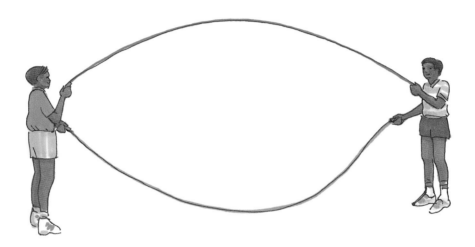

Here are some tips to keep in mind:

1. Stand straight.
2. Keep your elbows close to your body. Hold the ropes with your thumbs on top.
3. Begin turning small circles with the ropes stretched almost straight out. One partner then moves toward the other until the ropes touch the ground. Your hands should rotate between your nose and your waist.
4. Concentrate on smooth, rhythmic turning. Try counting one-two, one-two as the ropes hit the floor.
5. Watch your partner and point out problems you see.

Turning Practice

Once you have a steady rhythm, try changing speed, both faster and slower. While turning, try walking sideways in one direction, then back in the other. Walk forward and back. The more you practice, the more comfortable you'll be with your turning partner. When you turn with a jumper, watch his feet.

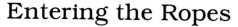

Entering the Ropes

Entering Double Dutch ropes can be a little scary at first, but it really isn't that hard. The secret is to watch the back rope (the one farthest away from you). It helps if the two ropes are different colors.

1. Stand close to the turner's shoulder. Listen to the rhythm of the ropes.

2. When the back rope touches the floor, enter with a big step and a big jump. You can actually begin your entry a little before the back rope touches the ground.

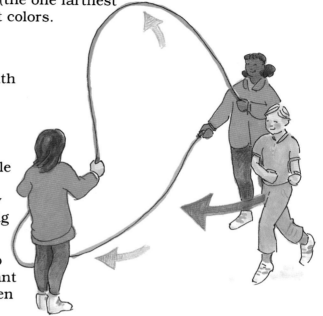

Remember when we were talking about the front-door and back-door entry with a single rope? In Double Dutch, you enter the rope farthest away from you by the front door, but you enter the one closest to you by the back door! That's why you have to take the first big jump to get in.

Above all, don't get discouraged! It takes practice to feel the timing and know when to enter. You might want to practice some single-rope back-door entries and then try it again with two ropes.

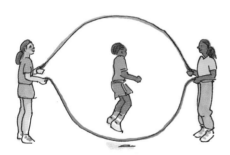

Jumping Double Dutch

The Basic Jump for Double Dutch is the same as for single-rope jumping, only a bit faster.

1. Jump on the balls of your feet, keeping your knees together.

2. Keep your arms at your sides, elbows bent. To keep from touching the ropes, clasp your hands across your waist.

Exiting the Ropes

The key here is to be quick and exit with a jump.

1. Face a turner.

2. Make your last jump slightly forward, toward the turner.

3. When you exit, aim for the turner's shoulder.

4. After you jump, exit quickly. Don't hesitate, but don't run out of the ropes either.

Double Dutch Tricks

After you're comfortable turning, entering, exiting, and doing the Basic Jump, you can begin working on some Double Dutch tricks. Many of the same tricks that work with the short rope and the single long rope will work with Double Dutch. Some tricks, like the Side-to-Side and the Side Straddle, work best after you've done a quarter-turn and are jumping with the turners on either side of you.

Jogging Step

This is just like running in place. In Double Dutch competition, this is the step used for speed jumping.

1. Enter the ropes and do a few Basic Jumps.
2. Start jumping with alternating feet.
3. Once you've got the hang of it, have the turners pick up speed!

High Step

Do a Jogging Step, but bring your knees up as high as your waist.

Turns

Try 360-Degree Turns in four jumps, three jumps, two jumps, and then one jump. Try turning on only your left or right foot.

Partners

When you jump with a partner, you and your partner enter from opposite sides. Once you're in the ropes, you can hold hands, do unison tricks, play leapfrog (that one takes some practice), or do dance steps. Be creative. Practice your routines without the rope first, and then try them with the rope.

Single Rope Inside Double Dutch Ropes

Take a single rope into the Double Dutch ropes. Face the turner with the rope behind you. Begin jumping the single rope in rhythm with the Double Dutch ropes.

More Friends

These are games for the whole gang!

Three Ropes, Three Turners

Three friends make a triangle, with each person turning two ropes. A fourth friend jumps in, does tricks, jumps out, and then goes to another rope. Move around the triangle this way.

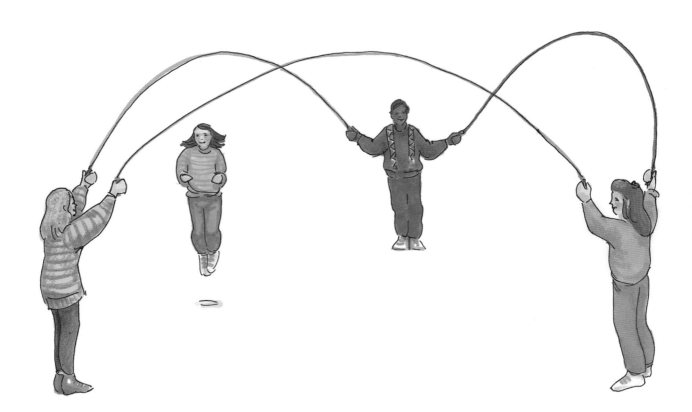

Two Ropes, Four Turners

Four turners stand in a square, with each pair's ropes crossing the other's ropes in the middle. Start turning at the same time. The jumper jumps both ropes at once. Once you've mastered that, try taking a single rope into the middle with you!

The Extra Long Rope

By using a rope that's 35 to 50 feet long (10.5 to 15 meters), you can get two loops going at once.

To Get the Rope Going

The turners turn the rope just as they would for the shorter rope, except that one turner begins to turn the rope a moment before the other. The idea is to make the turning rope into an S-shape.

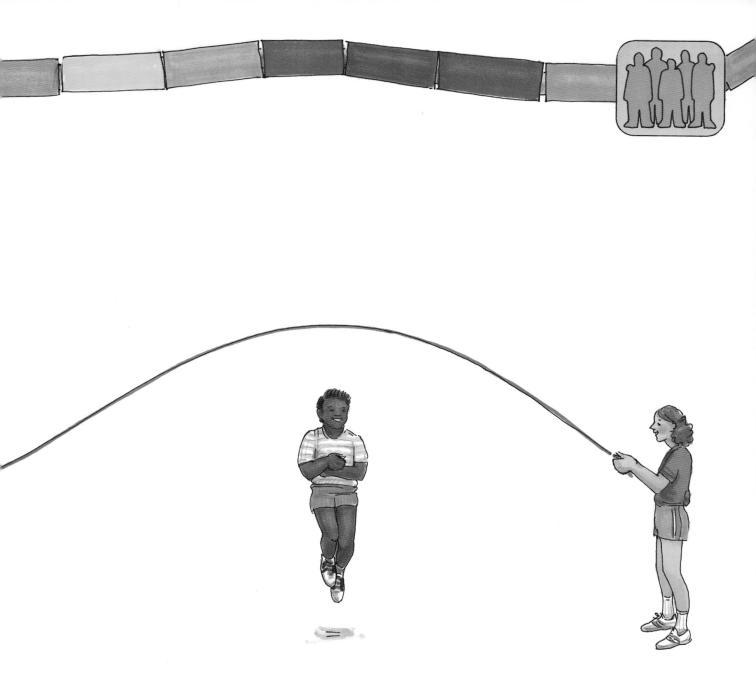

Entering, Jumping, and Exiting

This works the same way as with the shorter rope, except that the rope turns faster—you have to do everything a little quicker.

A Little Traveling Music

"Traveling" is a fun and exciting trick to do with a single rope jumper and three or four friends. The traveler moves down a line, jumping with each friend in turn. A slightly longer rope works best. When you stand on it, the ends should reach the top of your shoulders.

1. The four jumpers line up, a double arms-width apart.
2. Everyone begins jumping in rhythm with the fifth person, the traveler, who has the rope. Jump a little higher than usual, and keep a strong, consistent rhythm.
3. The traveler goes to the back of the first jumper and jumps with that person inside the rope. The traveler and the jumper should stand close together, only 6 to 12 inches (15 to 30 centimeters) apart.
4. The traveler moves to the space between the first two jumpers and jumps once, then moves on to the second jumper, etc.

Traveling Tricks

The traveler can do a figure 8 weave around the jumpers, moving in front and then behind the jumpers. The jumpers can line up in twos so the traveler can jump with both. The jumpers can move closer together so the traveler can jump with them one after another. Try your own variations!

Jumping Games

The single long rope is best for jumping games. Here are a few you can do. Most work best with three or more jumpers. If you don't have enough people, you can always tie one end of the rope to a tree or pole.

Follow the Leader

The leader runs into the rope and does a trick. The other jumpers each follow and try to do the same trick. When someone misses, he takes an end and the next person in line becomes the leader.

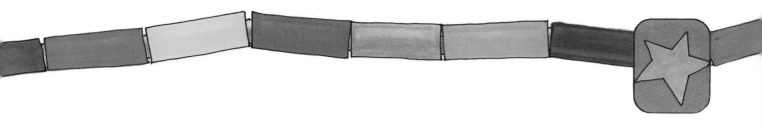

Running Through School

Each jumper runs through the turning rope without jumping and shouts "Kindergarten!" Then each one runs through, jumps once, and shouts "First grade!" Third grade is three jumps, fourth grade four jumps, and so on. If you miss, you stay in the same grade for the next turn. After 12th grade, you can go on to college by adding tricks to the jumps.

43

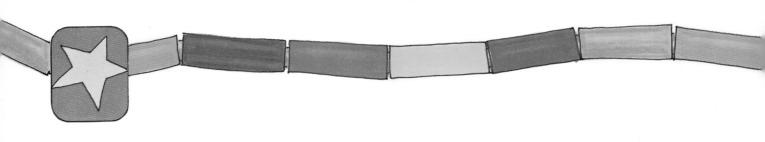

Baby's Cradle

The rope swings from side to side without touching the ground. The jumpers each take a turn jumping over the swaying rope until someone misses, or the jumpers can try all jumping at the same time.

High Water, Low Water

The rope is held stationary and each player jumps over it. When everyone has jumped, the rope is raised a little and the jumpers try again. If you miss, you're out.

High and Low Water are also terms that apply to ways of turning the ropes. High Water means to turn the rope 2 to 12 inches (5 to 30 centimeters) off the ground. Low Water means to turn the rope low over a jumper's head so she has to crouch to jump.

Snake

In this game, the rope is not turned. It stays on the ground, while the two "turners" wiggle it from side to side so that it looks like a slithering snake. The players try to jump over it without getting "bitten." If the rope touches you, you're out. The last person left is the winner.

Jump Rope Rhymes

Jump rope rhymes are poems composed by kids and rarely written down. Yet some have been around for centuries. Some have traveled around the world.

For a long time, adults didn't pay much attention to jump rope rhymes—until people like Dr. Francelia Butler came along. Dr. Butler collected jump rope rhymes for more than 50 years, from kids all over the world. She says that kids everywhere use rhymes as games, to keep time, and to express their feelings. So remember, when you jump to rhymes, you're part of a long tradition, one shared by kids everywhere.

MABEL, MABEL
Mabel, Mabel, neat and able,
Mabel, Mabel, set the table,
And don't forget the
Red Hot Peppers!
    (jump Hot Peppers until you miss)

DOWN IN THE ALLEY
Down in the alley where the garbage grows,
A flea jumped on an elephant's toes,
The elephant cried with tears in his eyes,
"Why don't you pick on someone your size?"

DICKEY

Dickey had a brother,
His name was Tiny Tim.
He put him in the bathtub,
To see if he could swim.
He drank up all the water,
He ate up all the soap.
He tried to eat the bathtub,
But it wouldn't fit down his throat.
Miss Lucy called the doctor,
The doctor called the nurse,
The nurse called the lady
With the alligator purse.

I'M THE WITCH

I'm the witch of Rotterdam,
Can you guess how old I am?
1, 2, 3…

I WORE MY CROWN

I wore my crown
To the alligator town,
I sat on a fence
And the fence broke down,
The alligator bit me
By the seat of the pants,
And made me do the
Hoochie-coochie dance.
  (do a wild dance)

GYPSY GYPSY

Gypsy, gypsy,
Please tell me,
What's my sweetheart going to be:
Doctor, lawyer, banker, thief,
Sailor, soldier, Indian chief?
*(repeat until you miss or make up
more occupations to add to the list)*

IPSEY PIPSEY

Ipsey Pipsey, tell me true,
Who shall I be married to?
A, B, C...
*(jump until you miss—the letter you
miss on is the initial of the one you'll marry)*

WILL I MARRY?

Will I marry, tell me so,
Is the answer yes or no?
Yes, no, maybe so, yes, no, maybe so...
*(repeat until you miss—the one you miss on
is your answer)*

MISSISSIPPI

How do you spell Mississippi?
M *(cross arms over chest)*
I *(point to your eye)*
Crooked letter *(cross legs and jump)*
Crooked letter *(cross legs and jump)*
I *(point to eye)*
Hunch back
Hunch back
I!

A, MY NAME IS ALICE

A, my name is <u>Alice</u>,
And my husband's name is <u>Arthur</u>,
We come from <u>Alabama</u>,
Where we sell <u>artichokes</u>!

B, my name is <u>Barney</u>,
And my wife's name is <u>Bridget</u>,
We come from <u>Brooklyn</u>,
Where we sell <u>bicycles</u>!

C, my name is _____,
And my husband/wife's name is _____,
We come from _____,
Where we sell _____!
    (continue through the alphabet)

50

BUBBLE GUM

Bubble gum, bubble gum,
Penny a packet,
First you chew it,
Then you crack it,
Then you stick it
In your jacket,
Then your parents
Kick up a racket.
Bubble gum, bubble gum,
Penny a packet.

BUBBLE GUM II

Bubble gum, bubble gum, chew and blow,
Bubble gum, bubble gum, scrape your toe,
Bubble gum, bubble gum, tastes so sweet,
Get that bubble gum off your feet!

CHARLIE CHAPLIN

Charlie Chaplin went to France,
To teach the ladies the hula dance.
First on the heels,
Then on the toes,
Around and around and around you go.
   (turn)
Salute to the Captain,
   (salute)
Bow to the Queen,
   (bow)
Touch the bottom of the submarine.
   (touch the floor)

I WENT DOWNTOWN

I went downtown
To see Ms. Brown,
She gave me a nickel
To buy a pickle,
The pickle was sour
So I bought a flower.

CALLING IN & OUT

Calling in, calling out,
_____ runs in when I run out!

ICE CREAM SODA

Ice cream soda, lemonade punch,
What's the name of your honeybunch?
A, B, C...
   *(the letter you miss on is
   your sweetheart's initial)*

ROBIN HOOD

Robin Hood, Robin Hood dressed so good,
Got as many kisses as he could.
How many kisses did he get?
1, 2, 3...
   (jump Hot Peppers until you miss)

EARLY IN THE MORNING

Early in the morning, about eight o'clock,
What should I hear but the postman's knock.
Up jumps _____ to open the door,
How many letters did she find on the floor?
A, B, C, D…
    (jump Hot Peppers until you miss)

I KNOW A BOY

I know a boy and he is double-jointed,
He gave me a kiss and I was disappointed.
He gave me another to match the other,
Now, now, _____, I'll tell your mother.
How many kisses did I get last night?
1, 2, 3…

APARTMENT FOR RENT

Apartment for rent, inquire within,
When _____ moves out, let _____ jump in.

HICKETY PICKETY POP

Hickety pickety pop,
How many times before I stop?
1, 2, 3...

A, B, C

A, B, C and vegetable goop,
What will I find in my alphabet soup?
A, B, C...
*(when you miss, make up something
that starts with the letter you missed on)*

I ASKED MY PARENTS

I asked my parents for 15 cents,
To see the platypus jump the fence.
She jumped so high she touched the sky,
And didn't come back till the Fourth of July.

MOTHER, MOTHER

Mother, mother, I am ill,
Call for the doctor over the hill.
In came the doctor,
In came the nurse,
In came the lady
With the alligator purse.
"Measles," said the doctor.
"Mumps," said the nurse.
"Nothing," said the lady
With the alligator purse.

UP THE LADDER

Up the ladder, down the ladder,
A, B, C,
Up the ladder, down the ladder,
H—O—T!
   (jump Hot Peppers until you miss)

I CAN DO A POLKA

I can do a polka, I can do a split,
I can do a tap dance, just like this!
1, 2, 3…

I LIKE COFFEE

I like coffee, I like tea,
I like _____ to jump with me.

WINDY WEATHER

Windy, windy weather,
All in together,
January, February...
    (jumpers enter on their birthday months)
Windy, windy weather,
They all run out together,
January, February...
    (jumpers exit on their birthday months)

GRANDFATHER'S FARM

As I went down to my grandfather's farm,
A billy goat chased me around the barn.
It chased me up a sycamore tree,
And this is what it said to me:
"I like coffee, I like tea,
I like _____ to jump with me."

ZOOP LA LA

Zoop la la,
Hey la la,
Zoop la la,
Hey la la,
Zoop la la,
Hey la la,
Zoop, zoop, zoop!
    (step on the rope on the last zoop)

56

TEDDY BEAR

Teddy Bear, Teddy Bear, dressed in blue,
Can you do what I tell you to:
Teddy Bear, Teddy Bear, turn around.
Teddy Bear, Teddy Bear, touch the ground.
Teddy Bear, Teddy Bear, do the splits.
Teddy Bear, Teddy Bear, give a high kick.
Teddy Bear, Teddy Bear, go upstairs.
   (walk toward one end of the rope)
Teddy Bear, Teddy Bear, say your prayers.
   (kneel)
Teddy Bear, Teddy Bear, turn out the light.
   (pretend to turn out the light)
Teddy Bear, Teddy Bear, say good night.
   (jumper exits)

I EAT MY PEAS WITH HONEY

I eat my peas with honey,
I've done it all my life.
It looks a little funny,
But it keeps them on my knife.
How many peas can I get on my knife?
1, 2, 3…

LITTLE BROTHER JOHNNY

I had a little brother
And his name was Johnny.
He played in the meadow
Where the frogs croaked funny.
He ran through the meadow
With a song on his tongue,
And he picked a few flowers
Just for fun.
How many flowers did he find?
1, 2, 3…

New Rhymes

Most of the rhymes in this book have been around for quite a while, but here are some brand-new rhymes. They came from Howard Zimmerman, a poet in Port Townsend, Washington, and from the kids at the elementary school in nearby Chimacum. We hope you like these rhymes and that they inspire you to make up your own.

CHOCOLATE BEARS

Chocolate bears and gingerbread cats,
All dressed up in whipped-cream hats,
Danced in the garden under the moon,
Beat sweet rhythms with a wooden spoon,
Whirling, turning, jumping to the beat,
Melting down to their ice cream feet.

When the baker ran to see,
They ran beneath the gum-gum tree,
Running in between the rows,
Tripping over ice cream toes.
There were 1, 2, 3...
    —Howard Zimmerman

BLACKBIRDS

Blackbirds, blackbirds,
Sitting on a wire.
What do you do there,
May we enquire?
"We just sit to see the day,
Then we flock and fly away."
By 1, 2, 3...
    —Howard Zimmerman

58

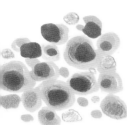

CHIMACUM CHEETAHS
Chimacum Cheetahs, turn around,
Chimacum Cheetahs, touch the ground,
Chimacum Cheetahs, show your spots,
Chimacum Cheetahs, hot hot hot!
    —Melissa Hoffer

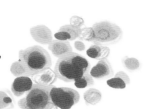

I MADE A WISH
I made a wish jumping rope,
I caught a fish jumping rope,
I gave a kiss jumping rope,
How many wishes (fishes, kisses) did I get?
1, 2, 3…
    —Dani Friedrich

WHALES
One whale, two whales, three whales, four,
One orca, two pods, three calves, more!
    —A. J. Sukert

BLUEBIRDS
Sixteen bluebirds sitting on a fence,
Flapped their wings and started to dance.
Upward, downward,
All along the line,
Brightly preened and looking fine!
Count 1, 2, 3…
    —Howard Zimmerman

If You Want to Know More...

Here are some organizations you can write to for more information about jumping rope:

American Double Dutch League
4220 Eads Street, N.E.
Washington, DC 20019

International Rope Skipping Organization
P.O. Box 3307
Boulder, CO 80307

Jump Rope for Heart Program
American Heart Association
7320 Greenville Avenue
Dallas, TX 75231

Books About Rhymes and Rope Skipping

Anna Banana, by Joanna Cole, illustrated by Alan Tiegreen. New York: William Morrow and Company, 1989. A fun book of 101 jumping rhymes.

Jump Rope Rhymes: A Dictionary, by Roger D. Abrahams. Austin: University of Texas Press, 1969. The big book of American rhymes, edited by someone who takes them seriously. Includes information on where the rhymes came from, as well as who wrote them down first.

Rope Skipping for Fun and Fitness, by Bob Melson and Vicki Worrell. Wichita: Woodlawn Publishers, Inc, 1986. Lots of skills you can learn, as well as interviews, history, and world jumping records.

Skip To It!, by Susan Kalbfleisch (Toronto: Kids Can Press,1985), and *Double Dutch Handbook*, by Susan Kalbfleisch and Tom Baily (Ancaster, Ontario: Ceta Publishing,1987). Two detailed, well-illustrated books about skipping, routines, and games.

Skipping Around the World: The Ritual Nature of Folk Rhymes, by Francelia Butler. Hamden, Connecticut: Shoe String Press, Inc., 1989. This is more of an adult book about rhymes, but it's a fascinating look at the way kids in 70 different countries use rhymes to express themselves.

Glossary

Here are some jump rope terms to remember. Some have already been discussed in this book, but others will be new to you.

Back Door—Jumping into a rope as it moves toward you.

Bluebells—When the turners sway the rope back and forth without turning it overhead. Sometimes called "wavies." This is the motion used in the "Baby's Cradle" trick.

Duck Jumping—Jumping in a crouched position.

Enders—Another name for turners, the people who turn the rope.

Front Door—Entering the rope as it moves away from you.

High Water—Turning the ropes 2 to 12 inches (5 to 30 centimeters) off the ground. Some rhymes call for higher and higher waters.

Hot Peppers or Red Hot Peppers—Very fast turning.

Low Water—Turning the rope low over the jumper so that she has to crouch to jump.

Salt—Very slow turning.

Up the Ladder—The jumper moves up the rope toward a turner. To move "down the ladder," jump backward toward the other turner.

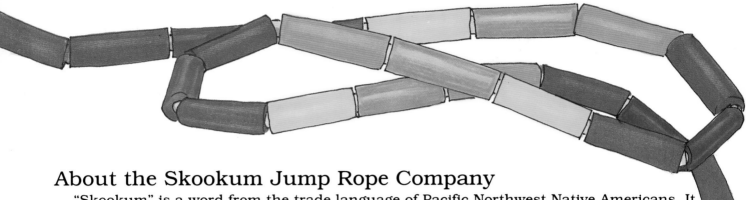

About the Skookum Jump Rope Company

"Skookum" is a word from the trade language of Pacific Northwest Native Americans. It means "well made" or "strong." The Skookum Jump Rope Company is a nonprofit business that is proud of the quality of its ropes and proud of the people who make them: developmentally disabled children and adults.

The Skookum Jump Rope Company began in 1982 in the special education classroom of Jim Westall, a teacher in Port Townsend, Washington. Over the years, the demand for our jump ropes has grown, and so has the company. We now employ 20 people and sell ropes to stores all across the United States and Canada.

The skill, good humor, and dedication of the workers at the Skookum Jump Rope Company make jumping rope a little more fun for all of us.

Acknowledgments

First, thanks to Bud and Sue Turner—the sort of physical education teachers we'd all like to have—for their knowledge, enthusiasm, and patience. We're also grateful to their amazing SCATS jump rope team in Seattle, who posed for photos and videos and proved that you really can teach old authors new tricks.

Bob Melson reviewed the manuscript and made valuable suggestions. Bob is a teacher, an author, and the coach of the internationally known Hotdog jump rope team from Kirkland, Washington. He's been a leading figure in the growth of rope skipping, and his enthusiasm for this project helped keep us on track.

This book could not have happened without the vision, patience, and persistence of the staff at the Skookum Jump Rope Company. They didn't quite know what they were getting into, but their commitment never wavered once they found out.

And, finally, special thanks to Dr. Francelia Butler, who took the time to discuss the history, meaning, and importance of jump rope rhymes with us. We were inspired by Dr. Butler's 50-year commitment to the poetry of children, a commitment expressed in the dedication of her book *Skipping Around the World*: "To all the children around the world who skip to the beat of human feeling, in the hope that their common yearning may move the world toward peace."

Bob and Diane Boardman
Port Townsend, Washington
January 1993

Send your favorite jump rope rhyme or trick to Skookum Jump Rope Company, P.O. Box 97, Port Townsend, WA 98368. Maybe we can use it in our next publication. Be sure to include your name and address.